Olga Korbut

Olga Korbut

A Biographical Portrait

BY
MICHAEL SUPONEV

PREPARED BY THE NOVOSTI PRESS
AGENCY PUBLISHING HOUSE, MOSCOW

DOUBLEDAY & COMPANY, INC.
GARDEN CITY, NEW YORK
1975

β
K

Library of Congress Cataloging in Publication Data

Suponev, Michael.
Olga Korbut: a biographical portrait.

Translation of Olga Korbut.
SUMMARY: A biography of the famous Soviet gymnast
stressing her career and including her suggested
exercises for making the body supple in preparation for
real gymnastics.
1. Korbut, Olga, 1955–   –Juvenile literature.
2. Gymnastics for women–Juvenile literature.
[1. Korbut, Olga, 1955–   2. Gymnastics–Biography]
I. Title.
GV460.2.K67S9613   796.4'1'0924 [B] [92]
ISBN 0-385-09498-1
Library of Congress Catalog Card Number 73–11636

Contents

Olga Korbut

1

A Triumph of the Will

The stands of the Munich Sporthalle sweep down in
great stretches, like the walls of some vast crater. And at
the bottom, in the arena, passions boil like lava in the
mouth of a volcano. The victorious women athletes
march by, heads raised high, striding as only they can—

legs extended, feet stepping firmly. At the side, the tears of the losers drop quietly. The stands, filled to the bursting point, explode now and again into applause, then lapse into a bewitched silence.

At the center is a small athlete in pigtails. Her size makes her last in line as the gymnasts, in close formation, pass from one apparatus to another. Later they will write about her: "Terrific!" "Astounding!" "Unprecedented!" She will be called the "queen of gymnasts." Poems will be dedicated to her. But right now she is exceptionally solemn and intense.

Her name is Olga Korbut. She is seventeen years old, is 5'1" tall, and weighs 94 pounds. Olga was born in the Soviet Union, in the west of the Belorussian Republic, in the small city of Grodno, on a street named after the famous revolutionary Kastus Kalinovsky. She speaks English well.

Olga finished secondary school in the spring of 1972, and has scarcely changed with the years: the little girl with ribbons who walked in leaps and bounds, is a little girl still. When she saw herself perform on the television screen, she burst out laughing: "What a silly little girl!"

Yet it was this girl, who conquered the Olympiad of 1972 with her astonishing courage and skill. No one else had gone through the complicated exercises Olga

Korbut demonstrated in the Munich arena, where, in spite of her years she proved that she was no novice in gymnastics. She has appeared in international tournaments in many countries, with varying degrees of success, invariably attracting attention, and it seems that her gymnastic repertoire is, in part, responsible for this.

All the elements that together make up a gymnastic composition are divided into three groups according to the difficulty of performance—A, B, and C. The most complicated are those in group C. At one time the Japanese virtuosos displayed elements somewhere beyond the bounds of normally accepted difficulty, and invented for them a special designation—"ultra-C." Olga's gymnastic composition contains more than a few of these "ultra-Cs."

But it is one thing to display super-complicated maneuvers in preliminary contests, and a completely different thing to appear before an Olympic audience—and for a novice all the more so. Olga had never appeared either in a world championship competition or at the Olympic Games. Nor would it have occurred to sports pundits to imagine that Olga and her trainer, Renald Knysh, would have decided to display such a complicated program at the Olympics.

In her composition on the uneven parallel bars Olga displays an element that even the specialized terminology of gymnastics has not yet found an expression for. She flies up to the upper bar, touches it gently with her hands, and standing bent over, begins to fall. A split second later she pushes away from the apparatus, shooting upward into the air. She seems to be on the very point of falling down, when, at the very last moment, she describes a sharp arc, and once again her hands reach the upper bar. Blithely she continues the composition.

At a memorable warm-up before the U.S.S.R.-Japan match, Olga performed one such maneuver that is still called the "Korbut element." The Japanese trainers immediately turned their movie cameras on her to be ready for the moment when the unheard-of element would be performed for the second time. Wisely Olga left it out of her formal appearance; it was plain that she didn't feel confident enough.

Later, in spite of the danger of a failure, Olga and Knysh didn't simplify their program by so much as a jot; instead they made it even more complicated, changing the composition and making it more striking. Once again at a warm-up Olga performed the "Korbut element." The vast hall reacted to it with restrained applause. At first it was all tenderness: "Ah, what a sweet baby!" Then there was enthusiasm: "But what is she *doing!*" Then during the actual performance the reaction was united: at first a thousand-voiced, "A-a-a-ah!"

that resounded identical in all languages; then a thunderous ovation that could not be contained even by the invention of the ingenious German engineers—the suspended glass roof vaulting over the Sporthalle stands.

In her appearances in each of the four events Olga demonstrated her own special "thing"—part of an exercise that had never been done by anyone. A flying leap forward is done nowadays by many gymnasts; it would be hard to surprise anyone with it. But a leap backward —that is something Olga alone can do! And in the optional exercises, which only a short while ago were considered one of Olga's weak points, she has a most unusual element—a leap performed while bent over forward, rotating on the chest. It is called the somersault—a jump in which the gymnast accomplishes a complete rotation in the air. But Olga comes down to earth not on her feet, as is usual, but on her hands, uses them to soften the impact slightly, lets herself down on her chest, and a moment later bounces up again on her feet.

The prescribed program for gymnastic competition is a predictable menu for gourmets. It cannot be called exciting—the inexperienced spectator gets bored during the prescribed program. But the Olympic spectator already knows that the real masters are capable of tucking special tricks that only they can do into the staid, tranquil format of the prescribed program. This is how

Olga Korbut looks at it: "We have a prescribed program, something like a piece of dictation in school. If you have to think—should you put in a comma or not? —you'll probably make a mistake. In such a case it would be better not to reflect, since the judges notice everything, especially your uncertainty."

In the Sporthalle the chief contestants among the Soviet young women—the girls from the GDR team, especially Karin Janz—wrote the "prescribed dictation" in a very precise hand. The judges gave Karin a particularly high rating for her performance on the parallel bars—9.85 points.

The Soviet girls were merely spurred on by such ratings. Olga took fourth place in the prescribed program, losing to Karin by only 0.35 points, while ahead of her were two friends, Tamara Lazakovich and Lyudmila Turishcheva.

The following day meant facing once again the gigantic roof, azure girders, and triple masts. Olga felt like nothing at all at the bottom of this vast bowl between the buzzing stands. At her side were the very tranquil Lyudmila Turishcheva and her trainer, Polina Astakhova, who was like a worried mama. She tenderly urged Olga into the arena: "Go on, there's nothing to be scared of! Just think we're having a normal rehearsal, talk yourself into it . . ."

A Triumph of the Will

And during the warm-up Olga did everything on the Munich mat as she had at home in Minsk in the Sports Palace, where she and the others had done their training for the last time before going off to the Olympics. There, on the yellow synthetic mat in the Sporthalle began a second, most difficult and happy day in the life of the closely knit Soviet gymnastic team.

Tonya Koshel leaped across the mat at a slant— gaily, lightly—and only at the very end of the optional exercises lost her balance and touched the mat with her hands. Of course she was not given a very high rating. Elvira Saadi came out onto the mat after Koshel and did her best to work more cautiously, more accurately. Her gentle lyricism won over the stadium; and though it rang out with applause, on the board there appeared a rating of 9.4. Then the melody of Bach's "Toccata," accompanied the lilting, rhythmic movements of Lyuba Burda, followed by Tamara Lazakovich, who embroidered an intricate pattern.

It is practically impossible to describe Olga Korbut's next compositions in the optional exercises; they cannot be encompassed by classical definitions. At first the stands grew quiet, then gasped in disbelief. When Olga finished the exercises the stands were torn apart by enthusiastic ovations. The spectators were conquered by Olga, who had just shown them a grasshopper, a butterfly, and herself—a girl who was not afraid of any somersault or pirouette, however difficult, and who could fly aloft into the air as though her weight were no more than that of a sparrow.

The rating—9.75—was disappointing; very naturally, the spectators began to express dissatisfaction, though still with some restraint. A little later, however, it became much louder after Olga was graded only 9.7 for a composition on the parallel bars, in which there were both an unrepeatable somersault and a jump that made the astounded audience gasp aloud once again.

It seemed as though all these points were not of the slightest concern to the Soviet gymnasts; it was a sight to see the bold, enthusiastic team. In the last and trickiest event—performed on a beam 10 centimeters in diameter —three girls, in addition to Olga, were given 9.75. And that meant a victory for the team. Thus, together with her friends, Olga Korbut became an Olympic champion for the first time.

The following day, too, brought her an ordeal such as she had never experienced in all of her seventeen years. At first the girl gymnasts in Munich performed the optional program twice—the first time, for the team as a whole; the second, for individual competition. For the first performance Olga received the highest score— 38.8 equalling that of the champion of the world, Lyudmila Turishcheva. But it was clear that Olga was capable of doing better since she had made a few minor, easily avoidable errors.

The second optional exercises began perfectly for Olga. She received .05 points more than the day before, adding that number for a jump and advancing into the first rank. Before her lay her own specialities—the bars and the balance beam. Looking back on this event it was calculated that if she had merely received the same scores she had for the first performance of the optional program, she would have had no equals in the all-around event.

Olga went onto the parallel bars calmly concentrating, waiting for a moment while going over in her mind the entire composition. Taking hold of the lower bar with her hands, she began the first flying movement and —caught her feet in the matting. A primitive blunder, severely punished by the judges. But it didn't end with that! This time, too, Olga performed her famous somersault excellently, but in the most simple elements she had accumulated so many mistakes that with the best will in the world the judges could not give her a rating of more than 7.5—a negligible score.

Olga left the platform falteringly, sat down on a chair, covered her face with her hands and burst into sobs. There was a tomblike silence in the stands of the

Sporthalle; all the knowledgeable spectators knew that the Olympic gold medal for gymnastics had just dropped from the hands of this sobbing young girl, so popular with the entire audience. Coincidentally, none of her friends was nearby—each was occupied with her own event. So Erica Zuchold, one of the major contestants from the German Democratic Republic team, went over to her, embraced her, and whispered something in her ear. Olga did not understand the German words, but this kind voice, the gentle, sisterly touch of Erica's hands calmed her down. When, an hour later one of the journalists at the press conference asked about the relations between the gymnasts of the Soviet Union and those of the German Democratic Republic, Tamara Lazakovich responded:

"We're all real friends. You could all see that."

Karin Janz added:

"I completely agree."

The television cameramen moved their cameras toward Olga. The director was merciless; he kept trying for close-ups of her face, wanting to pierce through her tragedy. Elvira Saadi, with seeming casualness, strolled between the camera and the arm chair where Olga was sitting to shield her from the penetrating television eye. Too late—the photographers were already running over.

The following day photographs of Olga sobbing filled the pages of the entire German press. Olga tried to ignore all that.

The hall applauded when she wiped her eyes and once again marched into the arena. The stands were anxious to see the athlete who, moving up to the apparatus, was able to wrench herself out of the "tragedy" she had just lived through, leaping lightly onto the beam and executing her backward somersault brilliantly. The judges, conquered, gave her a rating of 9.8. No one ever got a higher score for the workout on the beam except Olga herself—on the day of the finale.

Asked what had happened to her on the bars, Olga answered very frankly:

"I never thought that anything like that could happen. No doubt I just don't have enough experience. And I still have plenty to learn."

The spectators saw and understood everything. When Olga appeared in the Sporthalle for the last time, contending for the first place in the various events, the sympathy of the crowd was unanimously hers. That day became a day of new ordeals and of a genuine triumph. Olga won two gold medals. For the third time the spectators watched her backward somersault on the beam: once again it was performed with assurance, with striking stability, just like the one-and-a-half reverse somersault during the optional exercises. These were the parts of the program in which Olga had won her gold medals.

Before the optional exercises there were the parallel bars—and there the storm broke out. Munich newspaper *Sportkurier* described what happened:

"The smallest girl was at the same time the greatest. In the finale, in the individual events, 17-year-old Olga Korbut was the worthiest recipient of the medal. Twelve thousand hearts were hers when the international judges gave her 19.8 points in all, thus depriving her of the reward she deserved—the Olympian gold medal.

"For ten minutes the Sporthalle was filled with a frenzied whistling, but neither the umpire Matlokhov (Czechoslovakia) nor Bertha Villanché (France), president of the Women's Technical Committee of the International Gymnastics Federation, though invested with the highest authority, deigned to rectify it."

But what really happened? Karin Janz was the incontestable victor in the exercises on the parallel bars. She executed better than anyone else the prescribed program and displayed the most complicated optional combination, which included one unique element—the somersault between bars. The correspondent of the

Sportkurier was wrong in trying to reassign to Olga Korbut her gold medal.

But if Olga's composition were to be compared with the exercises of those women gymnasts who received scores equal to or near hers, that would surely be something to wonder at.

Attempts to clarify the point of view of the International Federation of Gymnastics led nowhere. Madame Villanché, who until recently was in sole control of the Women's Technical Committee, preferred not to appear at a meeting with the journalists. Appearing at the press conference in the name of the Committee was the gray-haired seventy-two-year-old Hungarian, Valeria Nad-Kherpikh, who energetically defended the honor of the uniform and vindicated the judges, while the president of the International Gymnastics Union, the Swiss Arthur Gander, stated frankly that he was doing his best not to meddle in the affairs of women's gymnastics.

At this press conference Olga was given a tornado of applause. She said:

"I knew I had made a number of errors in my performance. It is up to the judges to decide to what extent they are fundamental. I'm still too young to assess their actions."

But the most far-sighted commentators saw something more in this incident than the unfairness of the judges or their errors. The well-known sports observer of the FRG, Ingeborg Kollbach, wrote in a column headed: "The Risk Will Not Be Appreciated":

"In the 'contest' of women gymnasts preference is given to purity of execution, rather than to difficulty. This may lead to stagnation in a few years, since there is not a single gymnast who will not begin increasing the complexity of the exercises if she is not appreciated."

The controversy over Olga's performance did not lessen her popularity with the press or with her fans. The newspaper *Abendzeitung* came out with two big snapshots on the first page—a laughing Olga answering with childlike enthusiasm the ovation of the stands, and the Australian swimmer Shane Gould, weeping with happy excitement. The caption was: "There they are—the darlings of the Munich Olympics! Both have realized their golden opportunity!"

"This 155-centimeter 'doll' of the Soviet team executed a leap into the hearts of the public through her sensational performance on the bars."

Olga Korbut represented Belorussian Republic; a silver medal and two of the fifty gold medals awarded to Soviet athletes came to her. And she shared one more victory—the victory of the team.

A Triumph of the Will

What was the explanation for the outstanding success of Olga and her teammates? It won't be difficult to understand if we follow the Olympic path taken by the Soviet school of gymnastics.

The ceremonial opening of the Twentieth Olympic Games in Munich. The Soviet team enters the stadium.

Soviet gymnasts enter the Sporthalle. Members of the U.S.S.R. gymnastics team, from left to right: Antonina Koshel, Elvira Saadi, Olga Korbut, Lyubov Burda, Lyudmila Tourishcheva, Tamara Lazakovich, and the trainer, Polina Astakhova.

Munich. The Twentieth Olympic Games. Heads held high, the victors march in as only athletes can—legs extended, feet firmly planted.

The spectators were captivated by a girl with pigtails, who has just shown them a grasshopper, a butterfly, and —herself.

Dead silence throughout the hall—a foretaste of something never seen before.

Olga flies to the high pole . . .

A thrust away from the bar—and off into the air!

One of Korbut's famous somersaults!

Describing an acute arc in the air.

On the high pole once again.

First steps on the beam.

Composition coming up.

Holding their breath, the spectators follow Olga's performance.

A back somersault. In the entire world the first person to perform this movement—Olga Korbut.

Judges rate her performance 9.9.

2

In That School There Are Only Winners

From 1952 on, a new phase began in the history of the Olympic movement. Twenty years before the Munich Games, Soviet athletes appeared for the first time; ever since they have constantly been in the center of Olympic events.

Olga Korbut

One of the brightest pages in the Olympic debut of the Soviet athletes was the appearance of the gymnasts. It coincided with the change in the program for women's competition. For the first time, first place was taken individually and by the team. Previously, the medals were awarded for performances in individual events. As a concession to the past, some team exercises with ribbons, balls, and other objects were still retained, but after the Sixteenth Olympic Games in Melbourne they were given up altogether.

To many people the debut of the Soviet gymnasts in Helsinki seemed stunning. They won first place both as a team and as individuals, and performed splendidly in individual events.

At home in the Soviet Union, this success astonished hardly anyone. It was taken for granted. National confidence was grounded in the immense popularity of gymnastics throughout the country. It became compulsory study in physical culture lessons in the general school system. There were dozens of special children's athletic classes, in which children and young people from the age of eight to seventeen took up gymnastics three or four times a week. These schools were, of course, attended by the most capable children, selected by qualified trainers.

It was from such a school that there also came into

the world the first Olympic gymnastic champion, Maria Gorokhovskaya, who on the eve of the Fifteenth Olympic Games was just thirty-one.

No member of the original Soviet gymnastics team appeared at the Olympic Games in Melbourne. Their places were taken by representatives of the next generation; the oldest was twenty-seven. Female athletes gained the experience they needed in the international student contests and the friendly contests for young people, at the most important event in Soviet sport—the Spartacus Games of the Peoples of the U.S.S.R.—all leading up to the world championhsip.

The gymnasts of the "new wave" made a brilliant appearance at the Melbourne Olympics. Once again a victory was won in the team contests, while the first place as champion of the Sixteenth Olympic Games was won by Larisa Latynina as an individual. Two gold medals were also won in the exercises in individual events. These victories were won by Soviet women gymnasts in a far more difficult contest than in Helsinki. In the four years between the Fifteenth and the Sixteenth Olympic Games, the skill of the women gymnasts of Hungary, Poland, Czechoslovakia, and Rumania increased perceptibly as it was developed under the influence of Soviet schooling. Joint appearances in comradely and official competitions and the constant

Olga Korbut

consultation of the trainers aided the women athletes of the Socialist countries to approach the level of mastery of the Soviet women athletes. It was foreseeable that in the future the gap in their ratings would shrink more and more.

To be sure, Soviet women gymnasts at the Seventeenth Olympic Games in Rome established a record that will be hard to surpass: out of fifteen medals for different achievements that were won in individual competition, only one—the gold medal for exercises on the balance beam—was awarded to the Czechoslovak athlete Eva Bosakova. The all-around Olympic champion was Larisa Latynina once again, while first place for teams was won by the six-woman team of Soviet gymnasts, almost the same group as in Melbourne.

In those years Latynina was the incontestable queen of gymnastics. Charming, graceful, sure of herself, she crowned the performances of the Soviet women gymnasts in the championship series; her compositions sounded like a harmonious major chord. And together with her there appeared the elegant and always slightly sad, Polina Astakhova, whom the world of gymnastics called the "Russian birch."

Today too they are together, though one lives in Moscow and the other in Kiev. Latynina is the senior trainer of the Soviet scratch teams, while Astakhova is a "lead-out" trainer. This term calls for clarification. According to the strict, almost puritanical rules governing women's gymnastics in official championship matches, men are not allowed into the performance area. An exception is made only for piano accompanists. Even if a male trainer lives in the same house as the woman gymnast, even if he has developed a female champion, he is not allowed onto the platform of world competitions or of the Olympic Games. The reasonableness of this rule may certainly be doubted, but it must be adhered to. It was because of this rule that women "lead-out" trainers made their appearance. They have the right to be on the platform together with the female gymnast, to help her in readying the apparatus, and to give her support during warm-ups.

Let us go back to the sixties. It was then, in Rome, that the Czechoslovak team took second place; this circumstance played a not unimportant role in the future development of gymnastics throughout the world. The women gymnasts of the U.S.S.R. returned from the Tokyo Olympic Games after losing the title of individual winner for the first time. Vera Caslavska, the eminent Czechoslovak gymnast, became all-around champion. She beat the leaders of the Soviet team, Larisa Latynina and Polina Astakhova. Both these women undoubtedly had unique individuality, but what distinguished them essentially at the time was acute mastery evenly displayed in all four gymnastic events, irreproachable technique, and control over every one of their movements.

Caslavska's superiority consisted of a massive interjection of complicated elements into the exercises and in the higher tempo of execution. Against the background of her dynamic performances the other women athletes looked a little sluggish.

After the return from Tokyo, bickering about the course of future development of Soviet women's gymnastics had scarcely had time to flare up before everyone was literally stunned by the results of the national championship matches that took place in the Soviet Union immediately after the Olympic Games, in December of 1964. An unknown fifteen-year-old athlete from Vitebsk, Larisa Petrik, was winner in the all-around tournament. She won by only .105 points over her nearest competitor, but that competitor was the great and unconquerable Latynina. Never had so young an athlete won such a victory in the greatest competition in the country. Skeptics said the judges must have succumbed to the charms of youth, and were exceptionally well-disposed to Petrik, but unbiased specialists claimed the opposite: No concessions whatever were made to the youth of the beginner. And one not unimportant fact entered into that claim: Petrik's constant competitor was an athlete who was just as young—Natasha Kuchinskaya, from Leningrad. It was only a fault at one of the apparatus, caused by inexperience, that prevented her from contending for victory to the finish.

What distinguished Larisa Petrik and Natasha Kuchinskaya? Both emotional élan and passion, and above all the ability to combine complexity and speed to take the place of pedantry. This does not mean that Latynina or Astakhova were characterized by a dry, naked technicism. Far from it. Their performances were both brilliant and lyrical. But the masterfulness of the young girls, who seemed to be thinking of points least of all, was akin to inspired art, and so marked a step forward.

More than any other gymnast, Petrik had an acute feeling for music. By nature she is an actress, temperamental and impressionable. It was no accident that four years later, in Mexico, she became the Olympic champion in the optional exercises, and that to this day the "Gypsy" she executed at that time is still referred to as a masterpiece. Nor was it an accident that not long before Munich she left gymnastics and went on to the stage. It is hard to define her genre of performance today: It is a sort of symbiosis of gymnastics and ballet; a solid, organic alloy.

Natasha Kuchinskaya was called the "Bride of Mexico" at the Nineteenth Olympic Games; the words reflected the general rapture of her audience. Natasha also left gymnastics early. For a long time letters arrived in Moscow, to the editorial offices of *Soviet Sport*, a newspaper with a circulation of three million, with requests: "Give us back Kuchinskaya!" "For the love of God, do something so that Kuchinskaya will return to the arena!" But other gymnasts took her place.

Vera Caslavska was again the winner of the Olympic tournament in Mexico. She beat Petrik and Kuchinskaya, and all her friends. But the time for great new changes in gymnastics was coming. In the middle of the four years between Olympics the world championships usually take place. Then the center became the Yugoslav city of Lyublyana where all eyes were on the women athletes, who in Mexico had been given modest roles. A seventeen-year-old student from the city of Grozny, in the Northern Caucasus, Lyudmila Turishcheva, was the winner. That same Turishcheva, who had been a shy novice in Mexico, had fallen from the balance beam and taken only twenty-fourth place. At the Olympics she had been put in as an "ice-breaker"—she was the first member of the team to go up to the apparatus. There is no particular honor in this—on the contrary, the "ice-breaker" is a sort of sacrifice. The judges never give her a high rating, no matter how hard she tries. They reserve the really great points for later; and this is an infallible pattern. All the "ice-breaker" can do is simply not humiliate herself, not get distracted, but do her best for the team. Then, Lyudmila Turishcheva docilely "bore her cross," but in Lyublyana, to make up for that, she went out for victory and won, in a tough struggle with an equally young gymnast from the German Democratic Republic, Karin Janz.

Karin had created a fanfare while still in Mexico. There she took an honorable sixth place in the all-around competition. To this day the legitimacy of Turishcheva's Lyublyana victory is being argued. It is maintained that if Janz hadn't fallen in the final event—the balance beam—the outcome of the whole thing might have been different. There is, of course, no particular point in quarreling about this. Natasha Kuchinskaya in Mexico was also bucking for an important title, and also fell from the parallel bars and lost her chance to win in the all-around competition.

The favorites in the Lyublyana championship matches made an impression through the complexity of their compositions. Five years before that the Soviet gymnast Lyuba Burda displayed on the parallel bars a unique element invented by her trainer, Eduard Stuckman. This element entered gymnastic terminology as "Burda's twirl." In Turishcheva's Lyublyana composition there were *two* such complicated twirls. On the balance beam Lyudmila executed another exotic element—a forward somersault done without the use of hands; and she did it twice in a row! Karin Janz's exercises were a new departure marked by elements of extreme difficulty, not called forth merely by the intention of stunning the spectators, judges, and contestants. Hers was a new trend in the evolution of contemporary gymnastics.

At the official championship matches each team had a reserve participant. She was supposed to be ready to replace a teammate if the latter suddenly fell ill on the eve of the competition (in the course of the actual event no one can be replaced). The reserve contestant also appears before the judges to perform the exercises customary before the championship. Usually the trainers use this opportunity to familiarize the umpires before hand with the gifted young athlete they are placing their hopes on for the future. The reservist in Lyublyana was Olga Korbut.

Olga had already given a good account of herself in

the national championship matches of the Soviet Union. She had won the highest distinction in the supporting jumps. In those years practically every single gymnast executed the identical jump, "bending forward, bending backward," or as it was otherwise called—after the famous Japanese gymnast—the "Yamasita." Because of this pattern, everyone had begun to tire of this particular jump. It became rather boring to see the women athletes, as though copying each other, sketch exactly the same automatic design. Accordingly, Olga also did the "bend-two-ways" jump, but a little differently from all the others. Sharply pushing herself away from the apparatus, she literally hurtled into the air, bending herself double in flight and bending back with such force that she actually lengthened the trajectory of the leap. No doubt Haruhiro Yamasita would have approved of this way of performing his invention.

A real furor was produced at this championship match, not by Olga's leaps or by her first gold medal, but by the complicated elements proliferating throughout her compositions on the bars and on the balance beam. The excitement was polarized however. Some people were disturbed by the originality of Olga and her trainer. Here is one of the reactions:

"No matter how paradoxical it sounds, it is easier to teach complications than to elaborate a style. That is one of the reasons female gymnasts have been getting younger and younger so quickly: 14-, 15-, and 16-year-olds easily acquire very complicated elements that used to be extremely hard to learn—even at the age of 20 and 21. But that also threatens gymnastics: the appearance of such young people means the vanishing of femininity, lyricism, and expressiveness without which I—and I think many specialists and spectators—cannot even conceive of women's gymnastics."

This is an excerpt from the book *Balance*, by Larisa Latynina, who was at that time, the senior trainer of the national team of Soviet gymnasts. Meanwhile, Olga Korbut, who even then had a most complicated repertoire, appeared in Lyublyana merely as a reservist.

In those years an interesting process was taking place in Soviet women's gymnastics. Beforehand, in the '50s, national scratch team was made up basically of athletes living in the big cities—Moscow, Leningrad, Kiev. This was easily understandable. That was where the best trainers and the finest sports equipment were concentrated. But little by little representatives of the provinces began appearing in the scratch line-up. Tamara Lyukhina came to Rome from Voronezh; she was joined in Tokyo by Elena Volcheskaya from Grodno. In Mexico there were three girls from small cities—Larisa Petrik from Vitebsk, Lyudmila Turishcheva from

Grozny, Lyuba Burda from Voronezh. In Munich, on the Soviet Olympic team, there was not a single girl from Moscow, Leningrad or Kiev. Aside from Turishcheva and Burda, the Russian gymnast team consisted of the Uzbek, Elvira Saadi from Tashkent, the Belorussian Tamara Lazakovich from Vitebsk, Antonina Koshel from Minsk, and finally, Olga Korbut from Grodno.

The Belorussians were able competitors:

During the past few years trainers in Soviet Belorussia have achieved the greatest records in women's gymnastics. Beginning with Tokyo, there was a Belorussian girl gymnast in the line-up of the Soviet national team at each Olympic tournament. At the Fifth Spartacus meet of the peoples of the U.S.S.R., preceding the Twentieth Olympic Games, one of the sensations was the victory of the team of Belorussian female gymnasts and the winning of medals in the individual tournament —the gold medal of Tamara Lazakovich and the bronze of Antonina Koshel. It was in this republic, too, that the gymnastics school headed by Renald Knysh was set up.

3

The Man Who Made a Miracle

Knysh was educated at the Minsk Institute of Physical Culture, which annually graduates around three hundred trainers and teachers of physical culture for the schools of Belorussia. A school headed by Knysh is financed by the municipal department of national education, while the location, the gymnastic halls, and equipment are run by the trades-union sport society, The Red Flag. Its task, as of every Soviet sports school, is to foster the physical health of Soviet children.

Shortly before the Tokyo Olympic Games, Renald Knysh, whose name was still not very well known at that time, trained two women athletes—Tamara Alekseeva and Elena Volchetskaya. As the phrase goes, each one was better than the other. Tamara's optional exercises were particularly good, as was Elena's balance-beam work, while both of them—this was noted by everyone—made first-class leaps. At that time, when the majority of women gymnasts were trying merely to jump high and come down solidly, Knysh's pupils were making inconceivable twists and turns, and standing up afterward without a tremor. Both of them, one after the other, became national champions in supporting leaps. Volchetskaya was even taken into the Olympic Games; in Tokyo she not only took the eighth place in the all-around competition, but even got into the finals of the jumps, where she was fifth. Outstanding, for a beginner.

A great deal was expected of Knysh's school. But suddenly Alekseeva suffered a bad injury and in keeping with the proverb, "misfortunes never come singly," Volchetskaya fell ill. Two other of his pupils parted from their trainer—one married and had a child, the other moved off to a big city to study. Taciturn to begin with, Knysh turned in on himself completely during these days. "Why? Why?" he asked himself, hundreds of times. Why must he begin over again with something he had put so much energy into, set all his hopes on? He found the answer; he had been alone. Without help, without people who shared his own views, there was no getting ahead.

Knysh began looking for assistants, and found them in his own former pupils. The most faithful and the closest was Tamara Alekseeva, who had just graduated from Teachers' Institute. Elena Volchetskaya got over her illnesses and also came back to her teacher. Lyudmila Galitskaya, whose little boy could walk now, joined him. A teaching collective was put together. Not of course, in one day, and not without months of hard work.

Now Knysh's school is known not only in the Soviet Union but beyond its borders. His views on gymnastics seem unusual, and often downright audacious. They are free of all stereotypes and fixed ideas. Few people share these views, and Knysh does not try to impose his views on anyone. He prefers to demonstrate his ideas in action.

Knysh sums up his personal vision of gymnastics with extreme terseness: "Gymnastics—is acrobatics on an apparatus. Everything done on the mat, on the floor, can be done in principle on an apparatus also—on the parallel bars, on the balance beam, on the vaulting horse. Isn't that simple?"

Knysh's girls don't know fear. And he didn't find such daredevils—he turned them into daredevils!

Olga's development is no exception. She went to school, conscientiously doing her lessons and loving to play. There was only one thing that bothered her—she had the lowest marks in her class. On the other hand the physical culture teacher found her exceptional: Olga did all the exercises better than the others and ran faster than her tall girl friends—even faster than many of the boys.

Once the physical culture teacher took his ablest pupil to the children's athletic school run by Renald Knysh. Elena Volchetskaya was the one who dealt with beginners. "Just look at that gifted young girl, she can do everything; I think she'll turn into a first-class gymnast." This comment, made to Elena Volchetskaya, was Knysh's first observation on Olga.

So Olga began attending two schools at once—the ordinary one and the one for sports. A year later Knysh took the young gymnast into his own group. From then on pupil and teacher were always together.

Olga's trainer is someone who seems interested in nothing but gymnastics. He is eternally brimming over with ideas. An inventor by temperament, he has perfected dozens of improvements in the equipment. In his hall there is felt matting everywhere—felt around poles, felt layers, lumps of felt. The apparatus is wrapped in it, the floor is overlaid with it. The girls fall on it without the slightest risk of bruise or injury. There are no other precautionary appurtenances at all. Nor will you see any trainers there fussing about their pupils with trembling hands ready to pick them up the moment they fall.

Knysh also conceives new gymnastic elements which have become his trademark. This taciturn giant, with his close-cropped black hair and a sorcerer's piercing eyes, has accomplished a real revolution in gymnastics. He took a long time hatching the idea of performing a backward somersault on the ten-centimeters-wide balance beam. On the beam! A somersault! Is it even conceivable? At first no on believed in this idea of Knysh's.

But he began practicing it with Olga. Instantly critics popped up, declaring that circus maneuvers were quite unnecessary for athletic gymnastics. Knysh stuck to his guns, and when Olga performed this somersault at the national championship matches in 1969 the spectators gave it a rousing reception.

Knysh is called enigmatic because he doesn't like, or rather, simply doesn't want to talk about himself or his plans. He smiles and is quiet, and no one knows what's in his mind. Ask Knysh what he's preparing for coming tournaments and he shrugs his shoulders and answers evasively: "Well, something . . ."

Once Knysh was asked whether he had any ideas for any new, completely unknown maneuvers. "Of course, I do," he answered with an enigmatic smile.

"Who'll do them? Olga Korbut, perhaps?"

"Perhaps. But perhaps someone else. Or rather, there's still no gymnast who can do them."

"Where will she come from?"

But Knysh says nothing. A long time ago he laid down a rule—no promises, no advance information. He is averse to any fanfare, any publicity, and acknowledges one response only—action. In Grodno one of these actions was given the jocular name of "Operation Natural Selection." Knysh sent his assistants throughout the district centers of Grodno Province and went off himself on a search for gifted girls. In Grodno, he became acquainted with all the girls between the ages of eight and ten. Not just some, but *all* the girls. Then, he talked with their parents, trying to guess in advance just how their daughters would turn out on the basis of genetic indications. Who knows, this "operation" might produce just that gymnast who would be able to perform elements never seen before, whose configurations were only just then being worked out in the trainer's imagination. What was the answer to a second question: Could it be that there was an abundance of talented girls in Grodno, a small town fundamentally indistinguishable from any other? "He who seeks will find."

In the gymnasium where Knysh is engaged with his pupils, there are many small "witches." Here the supporting jumps don't land on the usual mats, but on rubber nets that toss the girls up practically to the ceiling—it's both safe and merry. That was Knysh's invention. Another invention has to do with adjusting the uneven parallel bars. To set her rod at the requisite width, the girl doesn't twist anything, she simply finds the necessary, familiar division on the dial face and turns the lever round without applying any strength.

This kindhearted, shy man is mercilessly demanding of himself and of others. He is tireless with the young girls, youngsters still infinitely remote from the gymnastic heights and about whom it's still quite unknown whether they will ever attain those heights. For the best of his pupils he is ready to spend nights and days in the gymnasium.

It is a pleasure to watch Knysh giving his lessons. In the choreographed exercises he turns into a "ballerina." From the side this looks rather comical, but there is no smile on the girls' faces—this is business.

People ask Knysh: "Why don't you have a choreographer in the school?"

Usually calm and reserved, Knysh bursts out:

"And where will I get him from? There is no one in Grodno, you understand—no one! And the choreographer I need is not a ballet choreographer, but a gymnastic choreographer! And there's no such thing in our city, so I have to be one myself."

"And a trainer in acrobatics?"

Knysh recovers his calm.

"There is no such thing and there never will be. A gymnastic trainer must understand all about acrobatics personally, no one can do it for him. And if he doesn't understand it, he can leave."

In Knysh, zeal is a usual quality. It's the norm. To nourish it a small piece of wiliness has been invented. A special bulletin is displayed in which each gymnast is given a rating on the five-point system after each training period. The trainer announces the score, but the gymnast herself puts it into the bulletin. It is by no means obligatory for Olga Korbut or Tamara Yerilina or Theresa Kashtelyan or Lena Korchagina to become a "work champion"—these girls have all successfully appeared more than once in national competitions for children and young people, but they enjoy competition.

They train alongside pupils from the preparatory group —rivalry in zeal involves everyone.

Knysh is insistent, even stubborn, but never to the point of foolhardiness. What an effort he made, with the help of local specialists, to compose optional exercises for Olga Korbut! He searched for an innovation for her performance. What was missing was some small resonant chord, unique enough for Olga's talents. Knysh went off, first to Leningrad, to the composer Yevsei Vevrik and to the choreographer Aida Selezneva, and then to the Muscovites, the ballet master Galina Savarina and the accompanist Svetlana Arefyeva. And it was thanks to all of them that the composition was created that produced a furor in the Munich Sporthalle and brought Olga the Olympic gold medal.

Knysh felt he was right; he couldn't be talked out of it. For a long time the gymnastic specialists were carrying on fruitless discussions about the primacy of complication in the exercises as opposed to the purity of execution. Knysh never got entangled in these quarrels, even though he too had a definite point of view. He did his own thing; logically, consistently, he looked for new ideas, thought out and polished new elements. Not everyone was receptive to his explorations. At times his pupils accused him of overrefinement; they got him very low scores. Some rejected Olga's style outright. Yet Olga is now acclaimed.

Knysh himself is far more tolerant. He accepts both the manly severity of Lyudmila Turishcheva, the gracious elegance of Tamara Lazakovich, the sunny optimism of Cathy Rigby and even the chilly athleticism of Karin Janz. He acknowledges the many-sidedness of gymnastics and sees in just that its strength and its unique attraction. For him the main thing is—hard work, creativity.

Knysh's imagination was beginning to move again in the most unexpected direction. One day in December he ordered his assistants to assemble in the trainers' room. As usual, after a moment's silence, he said in a low voice:

"It'll soon be New Year's . . ."

The trainers kept tactfully silent.

"So what should we do—go off home separately? Each one for himself?"

"What can we do?" someone asked cautiously.

"Now listen: New Year's we're all going to get together—the kids and the trainers, right here, in the gymnasium. We'll put up a Christmas tree, have a party!"

There was no need to insist. It took off. In the training periods first one girl then the other, leaping off the

A passage in the voluntary exercises.

A passage in the voluntary exercises.

A passage in the voluntary exercises.

A passage in the voluntary exercises.

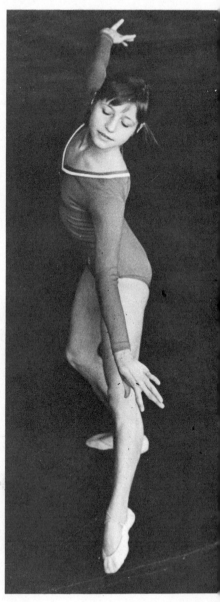

Storm the equipment!

This figure is called "bend and reverse."

An award well earned.

There they are—the Olympic awards.

Two Olympic champions—the Russian strongman Vasili Alexeyev and merry little Olga Korbut, among the most popular athletes at the Twentieth Olympic Games.

The daily routine of an Olympic champion. Olga Korbut and her trainer, Renald Knysh.

Knysh's school. Training on the bouncing sheet.

Knysh's school. Perhaps people will learn from these diaries one day about the first steps of Olympic champions.

The trainer and his best pupil.

Training usually begins with exercises for suppleness.

The trainer is always at her side.

One more somersault.

"Did I do it right that time?" Olga asks her trainer.

I'll rest a little, then once again . . .

Before working out on the equipment you have to limber up. Olga Korbut in the foreground.

One last piece of advice from the trainer.

Now—the voluntary exercises.

Worn out.

A moment's repose.

apparatuses, rushed over to her trainer and looking into his eyes asked him:

"And what d'you think if . . . ?"

"How about a costume?"

On New Year's Eve the gymnasium was unrecognizable. The apparatus was hidden away in the niches next to the walls. In the middle a pine tree was glittering with toys, its top nearly brushing up against the high ceiling. Cotton wool snowballs on very thin threads were hanging from it. A troup of rabbits, musketeers, gypsies and goblins were circling singing around the pine tree. Uncle Nick, hiding a smile in his bushy false beard, appeared in the hall and the children all yelled out in rapture:

"Uncle Renald! Uncle Renald!"

The prize for the best costume was given to the Wicked Witch, who no one recognized as the kindhearted, sweet-faced Tamara Alekseeva.

That was how the Grodno gymnastic school rang in the Olympic year. The New Year's party in the gymnasium, the somersault on the parallel bars, all the countless interesting new elements have only one origin—the constant effervescence of ideas, a sleepless fantasy.

To some people Knysh seems to be an iconoclast. But he's not that at all. Instead, he's the opposite—encouraging firm foundations, opposed to dogma. He casts doubt on gymnastic axioms and sometimes, of course, makes mistakes, but he is seeking, tirelessly innovating, constantly looking for something different in everything he sees.

Vincent Dmitriev, the well-known gymnastics teacher and world-famous trainer who trained the Olympic champions Larisa Petrik and Tamara Lazakovich, once said of Knysh:

"Knysh is, if you like, our conscience. When he is nearby it's impossible to be indifferent, to work at half-strength. We may take different paths, we may quarrel, but it doesn't matter—we still consider him our teacher."

There's no doubt that Olga is a talented gymnast. But without her trainer, with whom she has created her miraculous exercises, Olga would never have become Olga Korbut—an Olympic champion.

Knysh and Korbut are complete counterparts. The trainer is modest, quiet. Korbut is fiery, quick to take offense, wanting to do everything her own way, at times even shouting at her instructor, though she quickly gets over it. Knysh says that the relationship between him and his pupil is very complicated. Olga has the character of a small mule, and she had to be argued with day by day in order to persuade her that only an enormous amount of work, and not ability alone, could lead to success. But Knysh is far from complaining about Olga's headstrong nature. He thinks it is just these stubborn mules that produce sports personalities.

Olga came out for the national championship for the first time in October 1969. As a rule only girl gymnasts over sixteen years of age were allowed into the competition, and Olga was not yet fifteen. But an exception was made: the senior trainer of the U.S.S.R. scratch team, Larisa Latynina, saw Olga's exercises and decided that the girl would be entirely capable of competing with the ablest gymnasts.

Olga, the youngest and the smallest on the team, sent the spectators into ecstasy. She displayed extraordinary elements that were quite complicated, on the parallel bars as well as the balance beam.

After one match Olga was asked:

"Are you happy you took fifth place?"

"Oh, of course! I might even have taken a prize, but what a pity—I fell off the parallel bars!"

"And aren't you afraid when you execute such complicated turns figures?"

"At first I was. The somersault on the balance beam had never been done before, but now I'm not the least bit afraid."

A year later Olga won first prize in the national

competition—a gold medal as Champion of the U.S.S.R. in the supporting jumps.

In 1970 she was taken as a reservist in the world championship matches in Lyublyana. Olga successfully appeared before the judges' seminar and was highly praised. Suddenly she became terribly self-important; she turned up her nose everywhere, paid no attention to anyone—neither her friends nor the trainers—and quarreled with everyone.

But all this can be labeled faults of youth. A year later Olga had matured; her views on life had begun changing. The following season turned out badly for her. She was injured, fell ill, and for a long time missed her training.

After her triumphal performance in Munich, Olga, in a conversation with the journalists, said that without the support of her friends she probably would never have been able to win. The trail to the Olympic arena was opened up to her by the brilliant series of performances during the 1972 season: third place in the national championship contest in Kiev, a victory in the international tournament in Riga, first prize in the drawn match for the U.S.S.R. cup.

In sports there are not, generally speaking, any miracles. What wins is strength, the will to victory, thought, and inspiration, and Olga knows what inspiration is. Sport lovers were convinced of this by her composition on the parallel bars and balance beam—a soaring flight. The optional exercises in which gymnast's individuality was displayed to maximum effect were also a flight—a flight of inspiration.

4

When the Fanfare Died Down

In the autumn of 1972 there was an "explosion" in the postal department of the city of Grodno. The amount of correspondence arriving there grew so quickly that it was necessary to take on new workers. Letters, wrappers, parcels—all arrived for a single addressee,

(47)

even though the address was written in a great many different ways. Some of these were accurate and complete, but others were remarkably laconic: "U.S.S.R. Olga Korbut." Even such letters found their way to Olga Korbut. Throughout the year the city had never received so many communications from abroad as Olga did during the few months after the Olympic Games.

Olga is written to from every corner of the Soviet Union: from neighboring Belorussian towns and from far-off Kamchatka. The people she corresponds with abroad live on practically all continents. A great many letters come from the United States. She is written to in Russian by the students in the Slavic languages departments of American universities, and in English by people of various ages, interests and professions. This endless torrent of correspondence somewhat stunned Olga. She tries to acknowledge it.

"I thought I'd be asked for my autograph and picture. Of course there are requests for those, too, but most of the people who write me simply wish me well— they wish me good health, success in sports, and in general every sort of success; they congratulate me on my Olympic awards, tell me about themselves and don't even hope for an answer. And I feel so embarrassed about them, at not being able to find the time and the energy to answer every single one of them. And it's really rather insulting that I can't even read through some of the letters—sometimes I don't even know the alphabet they use, let alone the language."

In Munich there were some athletes who scored victories that were no less remarkable than Olga's. Seven gold medals to the American swimmer Mark Spitz, the unprecedented record of the Soviet wrestler Alexander Medved, who won the third Olympic tournament in a row, the astounding speed and the crushing blows of the Cuban heavyweight boxer, Teofilo Stevenson, the performance of the Japanese gymnast Mitsuo Tsukahari on the crossbar—all this was inscribed in the glittering pages of Olympic history.

Nevertheless, Olga evidently surpassed them all in popularity. Nor is it too difficult to explain this. Her magnificent skill, her innovations, her boldness, her simplicity and her personal charm, the drama that came out with her into the arena of the Sporthalle, and finally, the normal sympathy an adult feels for a younger person— all this made people from all the countries of the world well-disposed toward Olga. Television, after all, shared the Olympic games with millions of viewers.

Olga now recalls with a laugh the difficulties she had getting through the Munich shops. She wanted to bring all her relatives—her father and mother, her sisters, nephews and nieces—some Olympic souvenirs. "How could Auntie Ollie come back without a present?" said the seventeen-year-old aunt, not without pride. But buying anything was incredibly difficult. She was recognized in a flash, and something unimaginable happened: people asked for autographs, congratulated her, kissed her—it was impossible to squeeze through to the counter. Nor did the masquerade that she tried to arrange with a wig and maxi dress borrowed from a teammate seem to help.

If you said that Olga, her relatives, and friends were indifferent to this world-wide fame, who would believe it? It's all a question of just how fame and popularity are accepted.

On one of the opening days of the Twentieth Olympic Games in the Olympic Village, on Nadystrasse, 28, where the Soviet delegation was living, some guests arrived. Among them were famous singers, composers, dancers, and poets, who had come to Munich as tourists from the Soviet Union. A concert was improvised then and there on the little square in front of the 2800 block. It was attended by the Soviet athletes ringing round the square and their comrades from different countries who filled up the balconies of the adjoining houses. The last one to appear in this concert was Robert Rozhdestvensky. He declaimed his verses and finished up with a merry tale about the "Bronze Trumpets." The children roared with laughter listening to the ironic tale of the adventures of a hapless knight who had accomplished a mass of extravagant exploits, and had passed through fire and water, but couldn't endure the ordeal of the bronze trumpets of fame—"the knight lived and died, there is no knight any more."

The children laughed, then suddenly fell silent. The poet didn't address any of those present and recited the little fairy tale as though it were a mere entertainment. But the children understood that many of them would be called upon to pass through the bronze trumpets of fame, and that would be the test of their human character traits, a test that would be no less serious and difficult than the one awaiting them in the Olympic arena.

The bronze trumpets of fame in those days serenaded Olga Korbut hardly less loudly than the others. Would she be able to sustain their roar? Would the bronze voices not deafen her? It seems likely that she'll sustain it, in view of the support her family gives her.

Valentin Korbut fought during the war; he met it on home ground—in a village not far from the small Belorussian town of Kalinkovich. The Fascists had come by surprise. But the Soviet people were not about to submit to the bandits. They slipped out to the woods, made up partisan detachments, and rose in an armed struggle. Together with the men of his village Valentin Korbut took to the woods. He was fifteen years old—younger than Olga at the Olympics. Valentin did reconnaissance duty; together with everyone else he took part in the battle. More than once he fired at the Hitlerites trapped in the partisan ambushes; more than once the enemy's trains and motor transport blew up over the mines they had laid. In the flames of a genuinely all-national partisan struggle with the Hitlerite invaders who seized Belorussia, there was Valentin Korbut's spark, too. In one of the battles the young partisan was gravely wounded and shell-shocked. He was brought out to the "big country" on a special airplane and taken through the front lines to a hospital.

Valentin Korbut was discharged from the hospital when the liberation of his Belorussian homeland was nearing its end. He thought he would still have a chance to fight against the Hitlerites, but the staff of the partisan movement, already dealing with affairs of peace, decided otherwise. He was to be sent to Grodno to start living a peaceful life.

"But there are still Germans there," said Valentin, astonished.

"By the time you get there they'll all be gone."

Under the blows of the Soviet Army the shattered divisions of the Wehrmacht were hastily retreating westward. In fact, while Korbut was making his way to

When the Fanfare Died Down

Grodno on military routes in auxiliary vehicles, the Hitlerites were pulling out.

As secretary of the Grodno Young Communist District Committee, Valentin Korbut's worries were endless. He had to set up supply systems for the population, open children's schools, restore factories, and, principally, secure blood for those coming back home. He came to know a nurse at the military hospital set up in the city near the front. Their friends called them Valentin and Valentina and they soon married.

The Korbuts had more than their share of trouble. In Grodno today broad blocks of flats of well-built contemporary buildings are springing up, but at that time people in the half-destroyed town were looking for any sort of roof over their head. The Korbuts took refuge in a small wooden hut.

Little by little the family grew; four daughters were born. Valentin fell ill and could not work. Since for the previous few years he had been working as a practical engineer, Valentin was given a pension as a war invalid. His wife's shoulders were now burdened with new pressures. How she managed to do everything—work in a restaurant, feed and wash the children, attend to her sick husband—is hard to imagine.

Now the Korbuts' sad days are past. The elder

(53)

daughters are already married. The parents live together with the younger daughters, Lyudmila and Olga, in a spacious, well-built apartment. But there are definite rules left over from those difficult times—above all, work and industry are treasured, no respect is to be shown slackers, and a better future must be believed in. And in the Korbut family idle chatter and bragging are out of the question. Olga too has been brought up in accordance with these rules. In families with many children the younger ones must at times be given parental warmth and affection above all. Olga was the family favorite, but she was never allowed to become spoiled. At home she always had her duties, and even her Olympic gold medals haven't released her.

That's how things are at home. But aside from her family, Olga Korbut has a trainer who is generally referred to as a "second father"—Renald Knysh. To him the music of the fanfare and the roar of the bronze trumpets of fame mean nothing whatever. When he and Olga came back from the Kremlin, where the Deputy Chairman of the Praesidium of the Supreme Soviet of the U.S.S.R., Moteus Shumauskas, handed over orders and medals to the Olympic champions, Knysh congratulated his pupil, handing her a great award, the order of the Emblem of Honor, smiled and suddenly snapped:

"And now listen to what I'm going to tell you. At

the Olympic Games you didn't do even half of what you were capable of!"

Nor was Olga astonished. She knew that her trainer has never been altogether satisfied with her.

Knysh never reproached Olga for her silly failure on the parallel bars, never reminded her of the medals she didn't get, never took account of the points she lost, never cursed the judges. But on two points he demonstrated his own honesty. He spoke of the purity and stability of execution in the exercises. Knysh did not need any movie cameras in order to visualize the smallest details of Olga's performance in each of the four days of the Olympic tournament in each of the four events. He recalled very precisely where she bent her knees slightly and where she didn't stretch out her legs enough, where she made an unnecessary pause and where she didn't smile. The judges may think as they please, but he is convinced that Olga did her somersault on the balance beam worse than ever on the day she was given the highest score—9.9. For him, the Olympics represent the sum total of work extending over four years, the result of study and of creative inventions. Everything must be irreproachable. Knysh won't accept any other attitude to work.

And Olga agrees with this. She did, after all, say as much at the Munich press conference, though in other words. In the words of this seventeen-year-old girl, "I probably just don't have enough experience. And I still have plenty to learn." And the world has cheered on her learning.

5

The Daily Routine of an Olympic Champion

During the first few months after the Olympics a real invasion came down on Grodno—journalists, photographers, movies, television. Everything amused Olga. She willingly posed in front of the cameras, at the slightest request of the insatiable photographers and

(57)

movie cameramen she would change her dresses and her gymnastic uniforms. No matter what one says, after all, it's pleasant to feel like a movie star, even for a short time.

At that time the author arranged two interviews with Olga and her trainer.

"Olga, what are your first recollections and feelings about gymnastics?"

"Even now it's as though I could feel Elena Volchetskaya taking me by the hand, bringing me over to Knysh, as though I could hear her voice: 'Renald Ivanych, take this girl into your group. You'll see, something will come of her."

"Would you call that the happiest day in your life?"

"There are two such days. The first was when the other girls and I became Olympic champions in the team contests. The second was when I won the balance beam and the optional in the final contests of the Olympic tournament."

"And the saddest day?"

"August 29, 1972. That was when I fell from the bars and lost all hope of getting a good place in the Olympic tournament in the all-around."

"What is your favorite event?"

"Probably the bars."

"Do you believe in premonitions?"

"No, I don't."

"And do you carry a good luck charm?"

"Yes, I have a little toy hedgehog. I found it in Munich, and he's going to go with me everywhere."

"What's your favorite season?"

"Summer. But after all everyone loves summer, don't you think? Though maybe not. Pushkin loved the autumn."

"Do you like dancing?"

"I like modern dances, modern songs. But in general all that depends on my mood."

"What's your favorite color?"

"Red and white—that was the color of our costumes at the Olympics. And blue and green too."

"Your favorite aromas?"

"I don't know. But I love the smell of perfumes in general."

"What books do you like?"

"I like reading adventure stories, Conan Doyle, for instance."

"What do you think—to what do you owe your success at the Olympics?"

"Not what, but whom. To my trainer. Everything I have achieved in sports I owe to him alone."

"What do you respect most in your trainer?"

"His talent, stubbornness, his exactingness."

"Have you any sports ideal, anyone you would like to be like?"

"Lyudmila Turishcheva. I have a great deal of respect for her steadiness, her even disposition, her always being in control of what she says."

And with Knysh:

"In your opinion what qualities would an ideal pupil possess?"

"To my mind there's no such thing as an ideal at all. You always look for a pupil with good natural gifts— not tall, slender, springy, bold. Aside from that it's very important for a girl to be tenacious, capable of working, to pay close attention to the trainer's instructions and to grasp them quickly. Then it may turn out that you'll get a good gymnast out of her."

"Which of your pupils' qualities interfere with work?"

"The most disagreeable is an inclination to capriciousness. Laziness. A lack of purpose. Unfortunately, all these crop up quite often and are hard to overcome."

"What are your feelings when a pupil of yours is awarded a gold medal."

"Almost invariably I think it could have happened before if various obstacles hadn't turned up. Plans almost always turn out differently from what you expect. But I'm indifferent to medals."

"If you had a free choice of pupils, which of the contemporary women gymnasts would you want to work with?"

"Lyudmila Savina. I realize the name doesn't mean much. She's fourteen years old. She lives in Minsk. The girl has astonishing physical abilities and as far as I know splendid faculties of co-ordination. I'm sure there is a great future waiting for her in gymnastics."

"The international rules forbid a male trainer to be on the platform together with his pupil. Is that a hindrance for you?"

"In my opinion, there's no use discussing that question. The main thing is for all trainers and gymnasts to be subject to the same conditions."

"Your own daughter is no more than a year and a half old. Will she go in for sport?"

"I'll only be able to tell in six years from now when it'll be clear whether she has the gift for sport."

"Do your pupils' tears and smiles have any effect on you?"

"I try to pay no attention to tears. But smiles—that's something else again. They instantly make it more agreeable to work, you feel like giving the pupil more to do."

"Has there ever been a day when you were completely satisfied?"

"Never, nor is there any chance there ever will be."

"What are your feelings about the modern fashion in dress and hair-dos?"

"Perfectly bearable, and in any case I don't see anything wrong about them. And a lot of it I simply like."

"Do you like traveling?"

"No. I prefer staying at home."

"What are your feelings about hunting, fishing?"

"I'm absolutely opposed to them. I consider them a pure waste of time."

"What are your favorite cigarettes, drinks?"

"I've never smoked, I don't even know what a cigarette tastes like. In the way of drinks, I prefer fruit juices."

This is the strength of Olga's trainer. And it's quite understandable that he could endure what he called the post-Olympic chaos only with difficulty. He never got in anyone's way, and he accepted all this merry hurly-burly as something inevitable. Who knows what efforts of will power all this reserve cost him! In truth, what Knysh was thinking about, primarily, was the time spent so pointlessly.

For Knysh the four-year interval between one Olympics and another is infinitely small. His fantasy bubbles over with new elements as they form, elements just as unexpected as the somersault on the balance beam and the parallel bars. In addition, the gymnast must be persuaded that they can be realized. She must be forced to have faith in herself as being *the* one to realize them before she can be put through a long series of preparatory exercises, which must also be invented and tested in order to bring the athlete to the steady, assured execution of some unheard of element. But even that isn't all. The new element must be organically welded into the composition: It must not seem a foreign body, an artificially contrived trick.

"It's terrific, but nowadays the element is not bound up with the composition as a whole. It's the only thing that attracts attention. And the perception is lopsided—how did she manage it; how was it she didn't fall? Should this somersault be abandoned? No, the trick must be transformed into a component of the entire exercise. That may be more difficult, perhaps, than standing up and not falling, even though yesterday I couldn't even imagine anything like that could be done on the balance beam."

These are lines from Larisa Latynina's already quoted book, *Balance*. Knysh, who has been accustomed to listen to his own inner voice above all and take into consideration only his own opinion, unconditionally accepted the opinion of the twice-over Olympic champion. He realized that Latynina was right.

The somersault used to be the center of the composition: What happened afterward was not even looked at; it was perceived as a sort of appendage to the main maneuver. Knysh moved it to the very end. From then on complexity grew constantly, reaching its culmination in the finale: the backward somersault and then, all at once or, as the gymnasts say—in somersault tempo! —a jump in the reverse direction. The gymnast sinks down to conclude the exercise. And that's it! It is like the final beat of the kettledrums in the orchestra.

Because of this rearrangement the composition became irreproachably harmonious. But Knysh, with his eagle eye, could also discern in all this the technical subtlety too. Before Knysh's changes the gymnast had to sink down after the somersault on a 10-centimeter bar without swaying, which is exceptionally difficult. And now the forward somersault at tempo, in an uninterrupted movement, seemed to be concealing all possible mistakes, even though externally the link-up looked even showier. But even so, all Olga's remarkable capacity for work, her boldness, and her talent were required for her trainer's new invention to be realized in an impossibly short time.

Knysh understands perfectly well that on the road

Olga shows her family her Munich awards.

Lessons in the beginning class of the history faculty of the Pedagogical Institute.

In the library of the Institute.

Fifteen-year-old Olga Korbut, U.S.S.R. champion for 1970 in the supporting jumps, with her trainer, Renald Knysh.

The national competition for 1972.

The national competition for 1972.

The national competition for 1972.

The national competition for 1972.

The national competition for 1972.

In the national competition Olga was the bronze medal winner in the U.S.S.R. championship games for 1972 in the athletic gymnastics division, and at the same time a candidate for the Olympic team.

The joy of victory.

Lyudmila Tourishcheva and Olga Korbut during the Olympic competition.

"Daisies are my favorite flowers," says Olga.

from Munich to Montreal to the next Olympic Games, he and Olga together will have to solve such problems more than once; they will have to seek, find, reject what they find and seek again. But without that nothing will emerge onto the Olympic platform. The former Olga Korbut, from the days of Munich, no matter how much she was loved or how popular she was, won't be acclaimed in future Olympics by anyone unless she scales new heights, and for that, four years are practically no time at all. That's why Knysh sets such store by every single day, every single hour of training.

And Olga's worries have been added to since the Olympics. She attended the first class of the history department of the Grodno Teachers' Institute. When asked about a career, Olga still has no idea. Perhaps she will go with the expeditions through the steppes along the Black Sea, digging in search of priceless discoveries in ancient burial mounds. Perhaps she will become a school teacher or become an assistant to her trainer. At some time she may lead into the gymnasium a frail little girl who is going to grow into a champion, just as Knysh's first pupil, Elena Volchetskaya, once brought Olga herself to Knysh seven years ago.

No one knows as yet. But even so, there are only twenty-four hours in the day, and in them a place must be found for five hours of daily training, and for lectures at the Institute, for assignments in the library, for domestic affairs, for rest, without which energies cannot be restored for further training. There are meetings with athletes, with workers, schoolmates, students, soldiers, who all want to be told about the Olympics.

That is why twenty-four hours are just as cramped as four years. And why less and less time is left for music, of which she is very fond. Now before falling asleep Olga very seldom turns on her transistor. She herself doesn't know which music she loves best—classic or light, symphony orchestras or a super-modern band. Either, probably, as long as it leaves behind some echo in her heart. No doubt because gymnastics is in its very nature the music of movement, and Olga loves gymnastics more than anything else in the world. But now sleep comes to the exhausted Olga, and for a time the radio will stay switched off.

To be sure, there are other ways to live: abandon gymnastics altogether to be freed of some of her worries and hard work. One of Olga's relatives tried suggesting this to Olga: "What d'you need all this for? You've already got to the top—now you can be like everyone else. Don't torment yourself with training, slimming and diets, go to sleep when you feel like it, be cheerful, enjoy yourself!"

To Olga that means surrender. It means everything

must remain as before, and she cannot imagine that. There will be injuries, so hard to avoid in the major sports, and it will be impossible to eat her fill of cake and candy, because every extra pound of weight will drag her down to the ground in the midst of a flight over the bars or the gymnastic mat. And she'll have to go to bed early—she starts training, after all, at eight in the morning. She has to be in form every day, every hour.

Without that it's simply impossible. After all, Tamara Lazakovich and Antonina Koshel are not going to stand still; it wasn't so simple to win the first prize in Belorussia from them. Still less will Lyudmila Turishcheva be standing still, all of whose hopes Olga snatched in the all-around competition. And waiting for her in the contest for the world championship will be both Karin Janz, who shared a medal with her at Munich, and Zdena Dornyakova—the new hope of the Czechoslovak team, and the fair-skinned American, Cathy Rigby. She must prepare for the forthcoming world championship and for the coming Olympics because no one is simply going to hand her a place in the team—in the Soviet Union there are a lot of powerful female gymnasts. And one who tries to stand still in sports in order to take a rest will inevitably fall behind.

The Soviet weight lifter Yuri Vlasov, who broke the Olympic records in Rome, once summed up the essence of sport in two words: "Master yourself!" This is a law of equal validity both for the novice, who doesn't dare dream of fame and rewards, and for the champion, who has been through everything, knows everything. Master yourself—that means to repeat in training an element for the hundredth time that you cannot manage if it kills you, and that, as the saying has it, your very spirit balks at. Master yourself—that means furtively wiping away your tears after a failure and, as though nothing had happened, picking yourself up again for the next event. Master yourself—that means not looking back bewitched at the medals you've already won, but continuing straight ahead regardless of anything, and perfecting yourself.

Olga has already shown that she understands the meaning of these words. But she will have to go on mastering herself, in order to keep the love she won, in order to stay the girl she is known everywhere to be.

Olga's day, as you can see, is full of activity. Two training sessions, morning and evening, then study at the Institute, and her domestic duties. She is used to such a tense rhythm of life. There's one thing that bothers her, though—it's simply impossible for her to steal enough time to answer her countless correspondents. It would be easier if each letter contained only a "routine" request for an autograph or photograph. But many people, after all, ask for advice on how to become a gymnast, and Olga considers that very important.

But it's time to let her speak for herself . . .

"First of all, I should like to thank from my heart all those who have written me letters from so many different countries. These letters are very precious to me. They have helped me in difficult moments and have been a constant reminder to me of how much I owe, for all the joys I've shared with them.

"I get letters from the United States especially often. I won't hide the fact that this makes me happy, because after my trip to the United States I retain the most agreeable recollections of that interesting, unique country, its hospitable, friendly people.

"I know that the popularity of gymnastics in the United States has recently grown very appreciably. This surely means that some great gymnasts are going to make their appearance in America. I should be happy to see them on the platform and have no doubt that we shall have an interesting contest.

"I should very much like the marvelous world of gymnastics to open up before American girls, so that they will know the joy of moving their bodies and be given the happy opportunity of expressing themselves in movement.

"People often ask me—how can I become a gymnast?

(69)

That's the question that was put to me, for instance, by some girls from New York—Joan Powell, Laurie Lundin, Tamra Yatkin, Jeannemarie Giambron—by Katie Hower from Saint Louis, and by many other young American girls. I gladly take this opportunity to give them some recommendations; of course, I don't claim they'll be exhaustive.

"To become an expert gymnast on the highest level —what we call Olympic quality—is possible only after lengthy training, regular exercises, and attendance at a gymnastic school under the direction of a qualified coach. For me such an instructor, sensitive and wise, has been and still is my first and only coach, Renald Knysh. Everything I've achieved in sport I owe first and foremost to him.

"So—the gymnastic school. It is very important what you come to it with.

"It is one thing if you turn up there a clumsy oaf who has to start out from scratch, and quite a different thing if at your first training session you are already skillful, supple and—as athletes say—co-ordinated. And these qualities can be developed all by yourself, or even better, together with a friend.

"Any exercise, including those you do by yourself, must be begun by striding about. The object of this is to prepare the organism, the muscles, the joints, the ligaments, for the performance of the fundamental exercises, and for that you have to warm up thoroughly. How can that be done?

"It's best to begin by striding, then passing over gradually into a run. While striding you have to execute warming-up movements—leaning backwards, forwards, and sideways, putting your hands to your hips, doing a few falls, rotating your fists. It's useful to try dance steps in different rhythms—waltzes, polkas, mazurkas.

"When you've warmed up you can pass on to fundamental exercises in suppleness—stretching and balance. These qualities are absolutely indispensable for a gymnast in any one of the four categories that make up the program of the general competition that you'll have to acquire at the gymnastic school.

"Let's begin with learning the Little Bridge. For this you'll have to lie on your back, draw your legs up at

(71)

the knee, supporting your shoulders against the floor
with your arms. Then you straighten out your arms and
legs, so that the back is arched above the floor. Gradually, day by day, you have to try to bring your arms
and legs closer to each other, so that the Little Bridge
gets to be steeper and steeper. In this way the suppleness
of your back and a high mobility in the shoulder joints
will be developed.

"It would be good for a friend to help you perform
this exercise. She should raise you up by the shoulders,
and in that way strengthen the suppleness of the joints.
When you learn the Little Bridge you can pass on to a

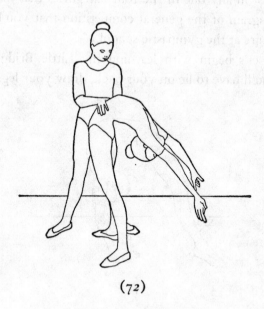

(72)

more complicated variant of it: After rocking back and forth on your hands and feet in the position of the Little Bridge try to stand up. At first it won't be easy; again, have a friend help you.

"Now let's try to develop suppleness in the opposite

direction. You can either stand or sit on the floor. Bring your stretched out legs together, hold on to the back of your neck with your hands and bend forward limberly. At first try to reach your knees with your head. Then try to reach your hips with your chest. Got it? Now, in the seated position, let's touch our chest to the floor, meanwhile spreading the feet slightly. Here, too, it's very useful to have a partner's help. When you've learned

how to make this bend while sitting down, try to perform the exercise in the same sequence, but now standing up. Don't forget—a friend can help.

"The next exercise is twirling your feet. Use a sup-

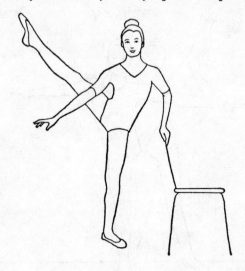

port for your hands. In home conditions this can be a table or chair. Hold on to it with your hands and stand off from it the distance of one big step. At first stand facing the support, and twirl your feet backwards and sideways. Try to make your movements as expansive as possible. Then stand sideways to the support and twirl forward.

"After learning the simpler variant of the exercise, go on to the more complicated. For this stand with your back to the wall and twirl your feet foreward and sideways. Then turn sideways and repeat the same move-

(75)

ments, adding some backward twirls. Here, too, a partner's help is in order. After learning this exercise you'll develop the suppleness of the pelvis and thigh joints.

"Later on we'll begin learning a component that in gymnastics is called the Cord, in all its different variants. In gymnastic contests you've surely seen it both in the optional exercises and in the combinations on the uneven parallel bars and on the beam. Squat down, place your hands on the floor and try to stretch out your legs—one

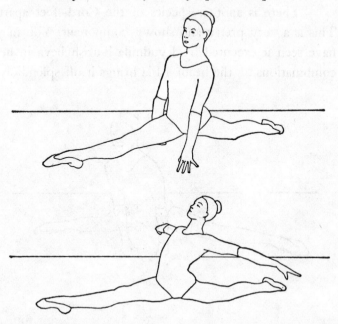

forward, the other backward. Make limber movements up and down. You have to learn how to keep your legs in complete contact with the floor—both knees and thighs. At first you won't be able to do it, but don't despair. The main thing here is—lots of repetitions, then you'll make it. Don't forget to change positions from time is time—if at first your right leg was stretched out forward, then move your left leg forward, and vice versa.

(77)

"There is another species of the Cord—feet apart. This is a very pretty and showy component. You may have seen it executed by Lyudmila Turishcheva in her combinations on the beam. Mila brings it off splendidly.

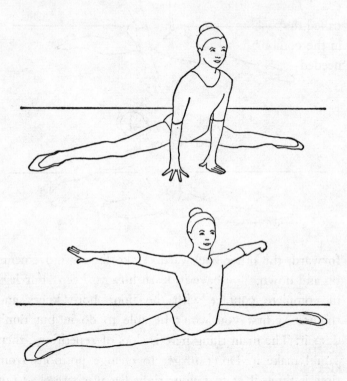

It is learned exactly the same way as the variant of the Cord with which we're already familiar. But you'll see that this is more complicated, and that in order to master it you need a lot of tenacity. But if you really love gymnastics you have to have enough persistence anyhow.

"There is one component in gymnastics that is called the Swallow. It's used in the optional exercises and in the combinations on the beam. To execute it, what is needed is a well-developed sense of balance. I won't

describe it, pictures will convey a sufficiently exhaustive idea of this component. I just want to remind you that in learning the Swallow, too, a friend's help is very useful. And don't forget to change the supporting foot from time to time. Among gymnasts, the ability to execute the Swallow standing on either the left or the right foot is very highly regarded.

"By learning the Swallow you're beginning to master an exercise that is very close to it—the side bal-

ance. You can see what that is from the above drawing. At first the side balance is learned with the aid of a support, later on without it.

"Every gymnast ought to be able to stand on her hands. She may enter a combination in any category.

Nor is learning the handstand really so hard. At first try standing on your hands by pushing yourself up with one foot and swinging the other. A friend will help you

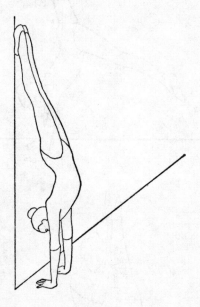

here, and she'll also be able to see to it that your body is in the right position. Then try to do the handstand without a partner's help, but by using the support of your feet against a wall. In that way you'll gradually advance to learning the handstand without help and without supports.

"There's a much-used component in gymnastics

called the somersault. My friend Lyudmila Turishcheva, for instance, executes this on a narrow strip of the gymnastic beam three times in a row, without touching the equipment with her hands. But that's already top-flight mastery, close to virtuosity. And for the time

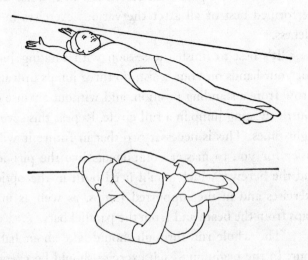

being we'll begin with something simple. You have to lie down on your back, stretching your arms up high. Then press your feet close together against your chest, hold on to your knees with your hands, so that you touch your knees with your forehead. Execute this movement slowly at first, and then, when you've become sure of yourself, do it quickly, snappily.

(*83*)

"When the first part of this exercise has been mastered, do a rock-and-roll a few times on your back, and finally get on your feet in a single, snappy movement. When you've mastered these preparatory exercises with assurance, you should be able to manage the somersault itself without any particular effort. It's an exercise that is performed best of all after the various exercises in suppleness.

"It's best to finish the session with rotating jumps. Put your hands on your waist, do three jumps upward in a row from a standing position, and without a pause do a fourth twisting jump in a full circle. Repeat this seven or eight times. This is necessary so that in future it will be easier for you to master components like the pirouettes and the Screws, which you'll need both in the optional exercises and in the supported jumps, as well as in the leaps from the beam and from the parallel bars.

"The whole run-through should take about half an hour. In the beginning each exercise should be executed seven or eight times; afterward increase the number of repetitions gradually to as many as 12–15. There are no special conditions for the exercises you do by yourself, as you have no doubt already convinced yourself. They can be executed completely in the most ordinary kind of room.

Daily Routine of an Olympic Champion

"These exercises constitute what may be called the ABC of gymnastics. But you'll need them later on as well, in the gymnastics school after you've become a real athlete. Only by that time they'll already be playing the same role as striding. Even now, for instance, I haven't forgotten them.

"The exercises I'm recommending are accessible to everyone. No special talent is required for them. On the other hand, what is absolutely indispensable is strict follow-through, effort, and stick-to-itiveness. Don't be frightened if they seem difficult in the beginning. That's only the initial impression. The important thing is not to retreat, you have to master yourself, as Yuri Vlasov once said very accurately about sport. This ability to conquer oneself is no doubt the most precious of all the things sport bestows on us.

"I am sure that learning these exercises by yourself or with a partner's help will shorten your path some-what to real gymnastics and will make it easier for your future coach to make you a real expert.

"And if this modest advice of mine can help any one of you to become a real athlete, then I can reckon that I've paid off a small part of the unpayable debt both I and my friends owe gymnastics for the immense and incomparable joy it has accorded us.

(*85*)

Olga Korbut

"I wish you success on your path to gymnastics. Be faithful to it to the end, never despair, and never forget —before you lies the joy of existence in the splendid world of movement."

Sincerely yours,
(Olga Korbut)

Now you have become more closely acquainted with Olga. This girl, so fragile looking, has undergone the most severe of ordeals in competitions of the highest class.

And she has undergone an even more difficult ordeal —the ordeal of fame. Global popularity has not affected her. Olga has remained much the same girl she was before her Olympic triumph. She still respects her rivals in sport and is close to them. She is still as curious and as keen, she contemplates the surrounding world with her eyes wide open, and never ceases being astonished at its richness and its variety.

In a word, she is still the same Olga we all love.

* * *

When this little book was already written, news came from Leningrad of the traditional match between the scratch teams of the U.S.S.R. and of Rumania. We give it verbatim from the newspaper *Soviet Sport:*

> Many contestants displayed original elements and compositions. But it is simply impossible to remain silent about the combination of Lyuba Bogdanova on the bars. Bogdanova executed Olga Korbut's celebrated somersault in a new variation, and concluded the exercise with a somersault and a double pirouette from a standstill to the topmost rung.

Olga Korbut's record for complexity on the bars was beaten. And that was done by Lyuba Bogdanova, who is two months younger than Olga. That same Lyuba, who together with Olga and some other girls, had prepared herself for the Olympiad, was not accepted for Munich. Sports connoisseurs obviously need not worry—gymnastics is not threatened by stagnation. Progress in sport can't be reversed.

It is significant that Renald Knysh takes the view that his best pupil—Olga Korbut—has not yet won all her Olympic medals.